Learning about Cats

THE MAINE COON CAT

by Joanne Mattern

Consultant:
Carol A. Pedley, President
United Maine Coon Cat Association,
CFF Breed Club

CAPSTONE BOOKS
an imprint of Capstone Press
Mankato, Minnesota

Capstone Books are published by Capstone Press
151 Good Counsel Drive, P.O. Box 669, Mankato, Minnesota 56002
http://www.capstone-press.com

Library of Congress Cataloging-in-Publication Data

Mattern, Joanne, 1963–
     The Maine coon cat/by Joanne Mattern.
     p. cm.—(Learning about cats)
     Includes bibliographical references (p. 45) and index.
     Summary: Discusses the history, development, habits and care of Maine
coon cats.
     ISBN 0-7368-0565-6
     1. Maine coon cat—Juvenile literature. [1. Maine coon cat. 2. Cats. 3. Pets.]
I. Title. II. Series.

SF449.M34 M38 2001
636.8'3—dc21   00-025774

Editorial Credits
Connie R. Colwell, editor; Linda Clavel, cover designer and illustrator; Katy Kudela,
     photo researcher

Photo Credits
Barbara von Hoffman, cover, 4, 12
Beverly Adams, 24
Beverly Caldwell, 6, 8, 22, 30, 34
CM Photography, 10, 28
Ron Kimball/Ron Kimball Studios, 15, 16, 18, 20, 26, 32, 36, 39, 40–41

1 2 3 4 5 6 06 05 04 03 02 01

Table of Contents

Quick Facts about the Maine Coon

Description

Size: The Maine Coon is the largest domestic cat breed. People often call them "gentle giants" because they are so large.

Weight: A full-grown male Maine Coon weighs between 13 and 18 pounds (5.9 and 8.2 kilograms). Females are smaller. They weigh between 8 and 12 pounds (3.6 and 5.4 kilograms).

Physical features: The Maine Coon is a tall and muscular breed. Maine Coons have large body frames. They have long, shaggy coats that are water-resistant. Maine Coons have long, bushy tails with dark ringed markings around them. Their ears have furry tips. Maine Coons' large feet have tufts of fur between the toes.

Color: Maine Coons can be many colors. These include black, blue, red, cream, silver, and brown. Maine Coon cats' coats can be solid colors. They also may have striped tabby markings.

Development

Place of origin: The Maine Coon is the first native North American longhaired cat breed. It is one of the oldest breeds in North America.

History of breed: Maine Coons probably descended from shorthaired American cats that bred with longhaired cats from overseas.

Numbers: In 1999, the Cat Fanciers' Association (CFA) registered 4,642 Maine Coon cats worldwide. Owners who register their Maine Coons record the cats' breeding records with an official club. The CFA is the world's largest organization of cat breeders.

Chapter 1

The Maine Coon Cat

The Maine Coon cat is one of the most popular cat breeds in North America. People enjoy these cats for several reasons. Maine Coons are large, friendly cats. They can make excellent pets.

Appearance

The Maine Coon is the largest domestic cat breed. Maine Coons can weigh as much as 20 pounds (9.1 kilograms). Male Maine Coons usually weigh between 13 and 18 pounds (5.9 and 8.2 kilograms). Females are slightly smaller. Most weigh between 8 and 12 pounds (3.6 and 5.4 kilograms). Maine Coons have sturdy bodies, muscular legs, and large feet.

The Maine Coon is the largest domestic cat breed.

Maine Coon cats do not reach full size until they are 3 to 5 years old.

Maine Coons usually do not reach their full size until they are 3 to 5 years old. Most other cat breeds are fully grown at 1 year.

Maine Coons have long, fluffy coats. The fur on their legs and undersides is long. The fur is shorter on their heads and backs. Their tails are bushy. Maine Coons have a ruff of fur around their necks. They also have tufts of fur on the tips of their ears and between their toes.

The length of Maine Coons' coats varies with the seasons. In winter, their fur becomes thick and heavy. Maine Coons' winter coats can be 2 to 3 inches (5.1 to 7.6 centimeters) long. They shed this longer fur during the spring and summer.

Personality

Maine Coons are friendly, good-natured cats. They seem to enjoy being around people and other animals. Maine Coons often make good pets for families with children, dogs, or other cats. Maine Coons seem curious. They want to be involved in the activities going on around them.

Maine Coons often are playful. Adult Maine Coons often run and play as kittens do. Maine Coons often climb on furniture and other objects. They also chase objects across the floor.

Maine Coons seem to enjoy attention from their owners. Maine Coons often follow their owners from room to room. They lay or sit near their owners. Most Maine Coons also seem to enjoy being held.

Maine Coons have unusual meows. Unlike other cats, Maine Coons make quiet chirping noises. Many people think that this small, high-pitched noise sounds strange coming from such a large cat.

Chapter 2

Development of the Breed

People are not certain how the Maine Coon breed developed. Several legends exist about this breed's history. These stories attempt to explain the Maine Coon's origins.

Legends about the Maine Coon

One common legend states that the Maine Coon breed developed from wild cats breeding with raccoons. This belief comes from Maine Coons' bushy, ringed tails and some Maine Coons' brown tabby coloring. But this story is false. It is impossible for cats to breed with raccoons.

Another legend says that Maine Coons descended from royal cats in France. In the 1790s, France was at war. Marie Antoinette was France's queen. She wanted to escape to North America during this war.

People are not certain how the Maine Coon developed.

Maine Coons' markings led some people to believe that the cats developed from raccoons.

The queen asked Samuel Clough to carry some of her valuable possessions to North America by ship. She planned to follow a short time later. Clough brought the queen's furniture, china, and six of her longhaired cats with him to Maine.

The queen never made it to Maine to claim her cats and possessions. She was killed during the war. Clough decided to keep the queen's cats in North America.

According to the legend, the queen's cats mated with native cats in North America. These matings produced Maine Coon cats.

The Real Story

Today, most people agree that Maine Coon cats first came to North America from foreign countries. Long ago, many foreign ships traveled to North America to trade. Ship captains often brought cats along on these ocean voyages. The cats killed rats and mice aboard the ships.

These cats developed features that helped them endure the ships' difficult conditions. These cats had large, sturdy frames. They also developed long coats that kept them warm and dry in cold, wet weather.

Ship cats often wandered ashore in search of food when ships stopped in North America. Many of these cats stayed in North America when the ships sailed home. These foreign cats mated with shorthaired cats native to North America. This produced Maine Coon cats.

During the late 1800s, Maine Coons were popular at cat shows in Boston and New York. In 1895, a Maine Coon named Cosie won an award at one of these shows. Cosie received the Best Cat award at the Madison Square Garden Show in New York.

After 1895, Persian cats began to arrive in North America from Europe. These longhaired cats became very popular. More people wanted to own and breed Persians than Maine Coons. This caused the Maine Coon's popularity to decline.

Many breeders still admired and enjoyed Maine Coons. They worked hard to keep the breed alive. By 1976, all North American cat registry associations recognized the Maine Coon as an official cat breed. Maine Coons then could participate in cat shows.

In 1985, the Maine Coon gained even more recognition. It was named the official state cat of the state of Maine.

Natural Breeding

Most cat breeds are the result of careful breeding. Cat breeders select cats with desirable traits or qualities. These physical features can include color, coat length, or eye shape.

Kittens usually have the physical traits of their parents.

Breeders then mate male and female cats that
have these traits. Breeders hope that the
resulting kittens will have the preferred traits.

The Maine Coon is considered a natural
breed. This means that it developed without
interference from people. Breeders did
not produce the Maine Coon. The desirable
traits of the Maine Coon are the result of
natural breeding.

Chapter 3

Today's Maine Coon

Maine Coons continue to be popular pets. Today, they are the second most popular cat breed in North America. Only Persian cats are more popular.

Development of Features

The Maine Coon's ancestors developed certain features over time. These features helped them withstand the difficult conditions of ocean travel. Today's Maine Coons display many of these features.

Maine Coons have thick coats and long, bushy tails. Maine Coons' thick coats help keep them warm. Their fur is soft and silky. This prevents their coats from tangling. Maine Coons can wrap their tails around their faces and bodies for extra warmth. Tufts of fur

Maine Coons have thick coats and long, bushy tails.

Many coat colors meet the breed standard.

between their paws keep their feet warm and dry. Maine Coons' feet also are larger than those of most cat breeds. This helps them walk over snow without sinking.

Maine Coons' ancestors caught mice and rats aboard ships. Today's Maine Coons also are excellent hunters. Their bodies are strong and powerful. Their square-shaped jaws help them grasp small animals in their mouths. Maine Coons' large ears and eyes help them hear and see animals around them.

Breed Standard

Judges look for certain physical features when they judge Maine Coons in cat shows. These features are called the breed standard.

Different cat organizations have different breed standards for Maine Coons. But most agree on several main standards.

A Maine Coon's body should be solid and muscular. It should have a long, smooth coat. The fur should be shorter on the shoulders and longer on the stomach. The fur also should be longer on the sides of the body. The tail should be long and thick. A ruff of fur on the chest or around the neck is desirable.

The breed standard also includes facial features. A Maine Coon's jaw should be square. The ears should be large and have tufts. The eyes should be large and set wide apart.

Almost any coat color or pattern meets the breed standard. The only color patterns not allowed are those that do not occur naturally. These include the colorpoint markings found in Siamese and Himalayan cats. These cats have light-colored coats with darker fur on their ears, feet, face, and tail.

Chapter 4

Owning
a Maine Coon

People can adopt Maine Coons in several ways. People can buy them from breeders or pet stores. People also may adopt Maine Coons from animal or breed rescue organizations. Maine Coons from breeders or pet stores may cost hundreds of dollars. Animal shelters or breed rescue organizations can be less expensive places to adopt Maine Coons.

Maine Coon Breeders

People who want a show-quality Maine Coon should buy one from a breeder. Most breeders carefully select their cats for breeding. Breeders also usually own the parents of the kittens they sell. This gives owners an idea of how the kittens will look and behave as adults.

People who want a show-quality Maine Coon should buy one from a breeder.

Many Maine Coon breeders live in North America. People who want to find a local Maine Coon breeder can attend cat shows. Cat shows are good places to talk to breeders and see their cats.

Breeders also advertise in newspapers and cat magazines. These ads are organized by breed. They list names, addresses, and phone numbers of breeders. Breeders also may have Internet sites.

It is important to find a Maine Coon breeder with high standards. These breeders are more likely to have healthy and well-behaved cats. Breeders should be members of the Maine Coon Breeders and Fanciers Association. Members of this organization agree to sell only healthy and well-behaved cats.

Pet Stores

People may be able to buy Maine Coon cats at pet stores. Most breeders do not sell their cats to pet stores. But pet stores may be able to recommend a local breeder.

Breeders with high standards are more likely to have healthy and well-behaved cats.

Animal shelters may have Maine Coon cats available.

Many pet stores are clean and sell healthy animals. But people should check out stores before they buy a pet. Buyers should visit stores and ask store workers where they get their animals. Buyers should look closely at the animals to make sure the animals look healthy and alert. The animals' cages should be large, comfortable, and clean. The animals should have plenty of food, fresh water, and toys. People should only buy cats from pet stores that have the animals' medical records available.

Animal Shelters

Many people adopt cats from animal shelters. These places keep unwanted animals and try to find homes for them.

An animal shelter can be a good place to adopt a cat for several reasons. Owners who adopt a pet from an animal shelter may save the pet's life. Many more animals are brought to shelters than there are people willing to adopt them. Animals that are not adopted often are euthanized. Shelter workers euthanize animals by injecting them with substances that stop their breathing or heartbeat.

Animal shelters also can be a less expensive way to adopt cats. Most shelters charge only a small fee. Veterinarians often provide discounts on medical services for shelter animals.

Shelters do have some disadvantages. Shelters often have mixed-breed pets available for adoption instead of purebred animals such as Maine Coons. People interested in adopting a Maine Coon can contact a shelter. They can ask shelter workers to contact them if a Maine Coon is brought to the shelter.

Another problem with shelter animals is that their histories often are unknown. Shelter

Breed rescue organizations can be a good place to adopt Maine Coon cats.

workers may not know anything about the shelter animals' parents, health, or behavior. Some owners may adopt cats with medical or behavioral problems. Shelter animals seldom have registration papers showing that they are registered with official cat organizations. Owners who do not have papers for their cats cannot exhibit them in most cat shows.

Despite these problems, many good pets are available at animal shelters. People who do not plan to breed or show their Maine Coon cats can find excellent companion animals at animal shelters.

Rescue Organizations

People interested in adopting a purebred Maine Coon may want to contact a breed rescue organization. Breed rescue organization members find unwanted or neglected animals. They care for the animals and try to find new owners to adopt them.

Breed rescue organizations are similar to animal shelters in many ways. But they usually specialize in certain breeds. They also rarely euthanize animals. Breed rescue organizations keep Maine Coon cats until people are available to adopt them.

Adopting a Maine Coon from a breed rescue organization can have some advantages over adopting from breeders, pet stores, and animal shelters. Breed rescue organizations often are less expensive than breeders and pet stores. These cats may even be registered.

People can find information about rescue organizations in several ways. Rescue organizations often have their own Internet sites. They also may advertise in newspapers and cat magazines. Animal shelters also may have information about breed rescue organizations.

Chapter 5

Caring for a Maine Coon

Maine Coons are sturdy, strong cats. With good care, they can live long, healthy lives.

Indoor and Outdoor Cats

Some cat owners allow their cats to roam outdoors. This practice is not safe. Cats that roam outdoors have greater risks of developing diseases than cats that are kept indoors. Outdoor cats also face dangers from cars and other animals.

Owners of indoor cats need to provide their cats with a litter box. Owners fill the box with small bits of clay called litter. Cats eliminate waste in these litter boxes. Owners should clean the waste out of the box each day and change the litter often. Cats are clean animals. They may refuse to use a dirty litter box.

With good care, Maine Coons can live long, healthy lives.

Some owners feed dry food to their Maine Coons.

Both indoor and outdoor cats need to scratch. Cats mark their territories by leaving their scent on objects they scratch. Cats also scratch to release tension and keep their claws sharp. This habit can be a problem if cats choose to scratch on furniture, carpet, or curtains. Owners should provide their cats with scratching posts. They can buy scratching posts at pet stores or make them from wood and carpet. Cats seem to prefer scratching posts covered with rough material such as indoor/outdoor carpet.

Feeding

Maine Coon cats need a high-quality diet. Most pet foods available in supermarkets or pet stores provide a balanced, healthy diet.

Some owners feed their cats dry food. This food usually is less expensive than other types of food. Dry food also can help keep cats' teeth clean. It will not spoil if it is left in a dish.

Other owners prefer to feed their cats moist, canned food. This type of food should not be left out for more than one hour. It will spoil if left out too long. Owners usually feed moist cat food to their cats twice a day. The amount of food needed depends on the individual cat.

Both types of food can be suitable for Maine Coon cats. Different cats may prefer different types of food.

Cats need to drink fluids to stay healthy. Owners should provide their cats with fresh,

Owners should brush Maine Coon cats once each week.

clean water each day. Most cats also like the taste of milk. But milk can upset adult cats' stomachs.

Grooming

Most cats do a good job of grooming their fur with their tongues. But some longhaired cat breeds such as the Maine Coon also need regular brushing.

Owners should brush Maine Coons once each week. Pure bristle brushes work best on Maine Coons. Synthetic brushes often create static. Combs work well on the thicker areas of the coat. Maine Coons may need to be brushed more often during spring. Brushing helps get rid of loose hair.

Owners must gently brush and comb Maine Coons. Brushing too hard can break off pieces of fur. It also can scrape the cats' skin.

The tip of a cat's claw is called the nail. Cats need their nails trimmed every few weeks. This helps reduce damage if cats claw on carpet or furniture. It also protects cats from infections caused by ingrown nails. Infections can occur when a cat does not sharpen its claws often. The claws then grow into the pad or bottom of the paw.

It is best to begin trimming a cat's nails when it is a kitten. The kitten will become used to having its nails trimmed as it grows older. Veterinarians can show owners how to trim their cats' nails with a special nail clipper.

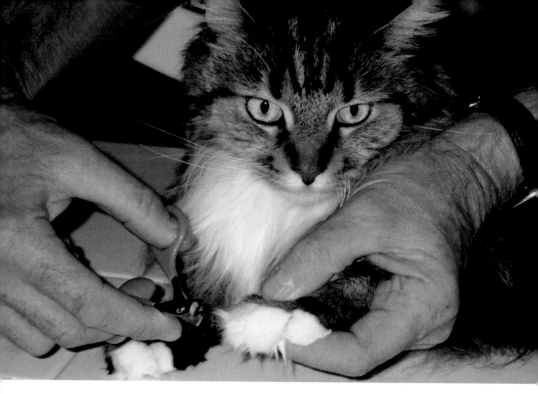

Maine Coon cats need their nails trimmed regularly.

Dental Care

Cats also need regular dental care to protect their teeth and gums from plaque. This coating of bacteria and saliva causes tooth decay and gum disease. Dry cat food helps remove plaque from cats' teeth. Owners also should brush their cats' teeth at least once a week. They can use a special toothbrush made for cats or a soft cloth. They also should use toothpaste made for cats. Owners should never use toothpaste made for people. Cats may become sick if they swallow it.

Brushing may not be enough to remove the plaque from older cats' teeth. They may need to have their teeth cleaned once each year by a veterinarian.

Health Problems

Most Maine Coon cats are healthy. But some health problems do exist in the breed. The most common is hairballs. Many longhaired cats have hairballs at one time or another. Cats often swallow fur when they clean themselves. This fur can form into a ball in a cat's stomach. The cat then vomits the hairball. But large hairballs can become lodged in a cat's digestive system. A veterinarian may have to perform an operation to remove these hairballs.

Owners can prevent hairballs by brushing their Maine Coons regularly. Brushing removes loose fur before the cat can swallow it. Owners also can give Maine Coons medicines that prevent hairballs. These medicines contain petroleum jelly. The jelly coats the hairballs in the cat's stomach. It helps the hairballs pass harmlessly in the cat's waste.

Maine Coon cats can suffer from hip dysplasia. This condition is common in large cats and dogs.

Maine Coons should visit a veterinarian regularly.

Animals with hip dysplasia have trouble walking. This condition can be inherited. It can be passed to a kitten from its parents. Maine Coon cats with hip dysplasia may need surgery to correct the condition.

Maine Coons also can have a serious heart disease called cardiomyopathy. This disease also may be inherited.

Good cat breeders test their animals for inherited diseases. They do not breed animals

that suffer from serious diseases. Good
breeders also tell owners if a cat's parents
had any health problems.

Veterinarian Visits

Maine Coon cats must visit a veterinarian
regularly for checkups. Most veterinarians
recommend yearly visits for cats. Older cats
may need to visit a veterinarian two or three
times per year. More frequent checkups will
help a veterinarian spot health problems in
older cats.

An owner who adopts a Maine Coon should
schedule a checkup appointment as soon as
possible. The veterinarian will check the cat's
heart, lungs, internal organs, eyes, ears, mouth,
and coat.

The veterinarian also will give vaccinations
to the Maine Coon. These shots help prevent
serious diseases. These include rabies, feline
panleukopenia, and feline leukemia. Rabies is
a deadly disease that is spread by animal bites.
Most states and provinces have laws that
require owners to vaccinate their cats against
rabies. Feline panleukopenia also is called

feline distemper. This virus causes fever, vomiting, and death. Owners who travel to cat shows often vaccinate their cats for feline leukemia. This disease attacks a cat's immune system. It leaves the cat unable to fight off infections and other illnesses. Feline leukemia is spread from cat to cat by bodily fluids. Cats also can be vaccinated against several respiratory diseases that cause breathing or lung problems.

Cats should receive some vaccinations each year. They receive others less often. Breeders have information on which vaccinations Maine Coons need. Cats that are kept indoors may not need all vaccinations. Owners should keep a record of their cats' vaccination dates. This record helps owners be sure that their cats have received all the vaccinations that they need.

Veterinarians also spay female cats and neuter male cats. These surgeries make it impossible for cats to breed. Owners who are not planning to breed their cats should have them spayed or neutered. The surgeries keep unwanted kittens from being born. They also help prevent diseases such as infections and cancers of the

Owners who are not planning to breed their cats should have them spayed or neutered.

reproductive organs. Spayed and neutered cats usually have calmer personalities than cats that are not spayed or neutered. They also are less likely to wander away from home to find mates.

Regular visits to a veterinarian are an important part of cat ownership. Owners and veterinarians can work together to help Maine Coon cats live long, healthy lives.

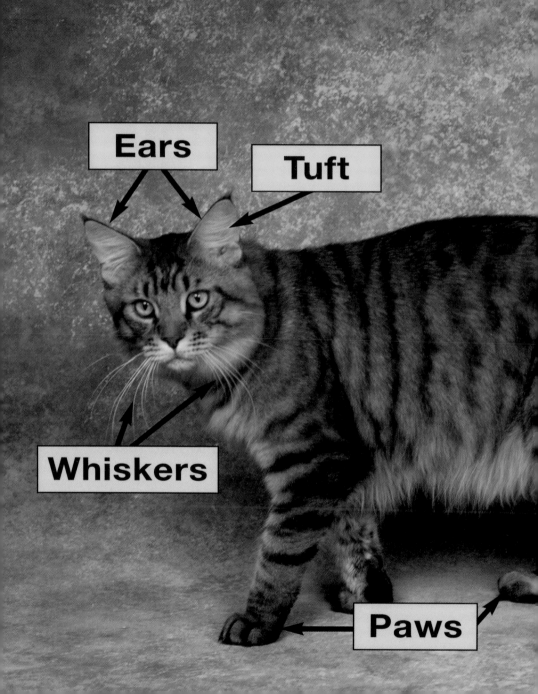

Tail

Quick Facts about Cats

A male cat is called a tom. A female cat is called a queen. A young cat is called a kitten. A family of kittens born at one time is called a litter.

Origin: Shorthaired cat breeds descended from a type of African wildcat called *Felis lybica*. Longhaired breeds may have descended from Asian wildcats. People domesticated or tamed these breeds as early as 1500 B.C.

Types: About 40 domestic cat breeds exist. The Cat Fanciers' Association recognizes 33 of these breeds. The smallest breeds weigh about 5 to 7 pounds (2.3 to 3.2 kilograms) when grown. The largest breeds can weigh more than 18 pounds (8.2 kilograms). Cat breeds may be either shorthaired or longhaired. Cats' coats can be a variety of colors. These colors include many shades of white, black, gray, brown, and red.

Reproduction: Most cats mature at 9 or 10 months. A sexually mature female cat goes into estrus several times each year. Estrus also is called "heat." During this time, she can mate with a male. Kittens are born about 65 days after breeding. An average litter includes four kittens.

Development: Kittens are born blind and deaf. Their eyes open about 10 days after birth. Their hearing develops at the same time. They can live on their own when they are 6 weeks old.

Life span: With good care, cats can live 15 or more years.

42

Sight: A cat's eyesight is adapted for hunting. Cats are good judges of distance. They see movement more easily than detail. Cats also have excellent night vision.

Hearing: Cats can hear sounds that are too high for humans to hear. A cat can turn its ears to focus on different sounds.

Smell: A cat has an excellent sense of smell. Cats use scents to establish their territories. Cats scratch objects or rub the sides of their faces against them. These actions release a scent from glands between their toes or in their skin.

Taste: Cats cannot taste as many foods as people can. For example, cats are not very sensitive to sweet tastes.

Touch: Cats' whiskers are sensitive to touch. Cats use their whiskers to touch objects and sense changes in their surroundings.

Balance: Cats have an excellent sense of balance. They use their tails to help keep their balance. Cats can walk on narrow objects without falling. They usually can right themselves and land on their feet during falls from short distances.

Communication: Cats use many sounds to communicate with people and other animals. They may meow when hungry or hiss when afraid. Cats also purr. Scientists do not know exactly what causes cats to make this sound. Cats often purr when they are relaxed. But they also may purr when they are sick or in pain.

Words to Know

breeder (BREED-ur)—someone who breeds and raises cats or other animals

breed standard (BREED STAN-durd)—specific physical features that judges look for in a breed at a cat show

estrus (ESS-truss)—a physical state of a female cat during which she will mate with a male cat; estrus also is known as "heat."

euthanize (YOO-thuh-nize)—to painlessly put an animal to death by injecting it with a substance that stops its breathing or heartbeat

neuter (NOO-tur)—to remove a male animal's testicles so it cannot reproduce

spay (SPAY)—to remove a female animal's uterus and ovaries so it cannot reproduce

tabby (TAB-ee)—a cat with a striped coat

vaccination (vak-suh-NAY-shuhn)—a shot of medicine that protects an animal from disease

veterinarian (vet-ur-uh-NER-ee-uhn)—a doctor who is trained to treat the illnesses and injuries of animals

To Learn More

Daly, Carol Himsel. *Maine Coon Cats: Everything about Purchase, Care, Nutrition, Reproduction, Diseases, and Behavior.* A Complete Pet Owner's Manual. Hauppauge, N.Y.: Barron's, 1995.

Greene, Abigail. *Guide to Owning a Maine Coon Cat.* Popular Cat Library. Philadelphia: Chelsea House Publishers, 1999.

Kallen, Stuart A. *Maine Coon Cats.* Checkerboard Animal Library. Edina, Minn.: Abdo & Daughters, 1996.

Quasha, Jennifer. *Maine Coon Cats.* Kid's Cat Library. New York: PowerKids Press, 2000.

Stone, Lynn M. *Maine Coon Cats.* Read All about Cats. Vero Beach, Fla.: Rourke, 1999.

You can read articles about Maine Coons in *Cat Fancy* and *Cats* magazines.

Useful Addresses

American Cat Association (ACA)
8101 Katherine Avenue
Panorama City, CA 91402

Canadian Cat Association (CCA)
220 Advance Boulevard
Suite 101
Brampton, ON L6T 4J5
Canada

Cat Fanciers' Association (CFA)
P.O. Box 1005
Manasquan, NJ 08736

The International Cat Association (TICA)
P.O. Box 2684
Harlingen, TX 78551

**Maine Coon Breeders and Fanciers
    Association (MCBFA)**
P.O. Box 18981
Boulder, CO 80308

Internet Sites

American Veterinary Medical Association Presents—Care for Pets
http://www.avma.org/care4pets

Canadian Cat Association (CCA)
http://www.cca-afc.com

Cat Fanciers' Association (CFA)
http://www.cfainc.org

Cat Fancy
http://www.animalnetwork.com/cats/default.asp

The International Cat Association (TICA)
http://www.tica.org

United Maine Coon Cat Association (UMCCA)
http://www.cffinc.org/umcca/main.htm

Index

animal shelter, 21, 25–27

breeder, 14, 15, 21, 23, 27, 36, 37, 38
breed rescue organization, 21, 27
brushing, 32, 33, 34, 35

cat shows, 13, 14, 19, 23, 26, 38
coat, 8, 9, 13, 17, 19, 33, 37
color, 11, 14, 19

dental care, 34–35
diet, 31

feeding, 31–32
feline leukemia, 37, 38
feline panleukopenia, 37

grooming, 32–33

hairball, 35
hip dysplasia, 35, 36

litter box, 29

neutered cats, 38, 39

personality, 9, 39

rabies, 37
registration papers, 26
ruff, 8, 19

scratching posts, 30, 31
spayed cats, 38, 39

vaccinations, 37, 38
veterinarian, 25, 33, 35, 37–39

DATE DUE